ACTION SPORTS
# IN-LINE SKATING

**Joe Herran and Ron Thomas**

CHELSEA HOUSE
PUBLISHERS
A Haights Cross Communications ✈ Company
**Philadelphia**

This edition first published in 2003 in the United States of America by Chelsea House Publishers, a subsidiary of Haights Cross Communications.

Chelsea House Publishers
1974 Sproul Road, Suite 400
Broomall, PA 19008-0914

The Chelsea House world wide web address is www.chelseahouse.com

Library of Congress Cataloging-in-Publication Data Applied for.
ISBN 0-7910-6999-0

First published in 2002 by
MACMILLAN EDUCATION AUSTRALIA PTY LTD
627 Chapel Street, South Yarra, Australia, 3141

Copyright © Joe Herran and Ron Thomas 2002
Copyright in photographs © individual photographers as credited
Edited by Miriana Dasovic
Text design by Karen Young
Cover design by Karen Young
Illustrations by Nives Porcellato and Andy Craig
Page layout by Raul Diche
Photo research by Legend Images

Printed in China

**Acknowledgements**
The authors wish to acknowledge and thank Jodie Tyler for her assistance and advice in the writing of this book. Also James O'Connor, founder of the Australian Rollerblading Website, an online magazine found at www.rollerblading.com.au.

Cover photo: In-line skater, courtesy of Sport the library.

AAP/AP Photo/Cesar Rangel, p. 29 (left); AAP Image/Ben Margot, p. 27 (left); Australian Picture Library/Empics, pp. 18 (left), 30 (right); Getty Images/Allsport, pp. 8–9, 25, 29 (right); Getty Images/Photodisc, p. 6; National Museum of Roller Skating, Lincoln, Nebraska, p. 28; Dale Mann/Retrospect, pp. 14, 15, 19 (right and bottom), 20 (left); Sporting Images, p. 4; Sport the library, pp. 5, 10, 11, 12, 13, 16 (top), 17, 18 (right), 19 (top), 20–21 (all), 22, 24, 26, 27 (right), 30 (left).

While every care has been taken to trace and acknowledge copyright the publisher tenders their apologies for any accidental infringement where copyright has proved untraceable.

# CONTENTS

# INTRODUCTION

In this book you will read about:

- in-line skates
- the gear used by skaters
- safety measures used to keep skaters safe
- some basic in-line skating skills
- tricks and stunts performed by experienced and professional skaters on the streets or in the **halfpipe**
- some of the top in-line skaters in competition today
- the history of the sport from its beginnings in the 1980s.

## In the beginning

In-line skates were developed in the 1980s by ice-hockey players who wanted to continue training during the summer months. Soon afterwards snow skiers, snowboarders and people from many other sports discovered in-line skating. They found that it kept them fit, and built strength and stamina for their favorite sports. In-line skating soon became a popular sport in itself, as children and adults alike enjoyed its speed and excitement.

## In-line skating today

New sports, such as aggressive in-line skating, have grown from in-line skating. Aggressive in-line skaters have borrowed skills and techniques from skateboarders to develop two types of in-line skating: street skating and **vert** skating. Like skateboarders, street-style in-line skaters jump over and **grind** across just about any obstacle imaginable. Vert in-line skaters do tricks in the huge halfpipe.

> **⊿ Warning**
>
> This is not a how-to book for aspiring in-line skaters. It is intended as an introduction to the exciting world of in-line skating, and a look at where the sport has come from and where it is heading.

# WHAT IS IN-LINE SKATING?

In-line skating uses a pair of skates with a single row of wheels on each skate. In-line skating can be done on streets and roads or in **skate parks**. There are two main types of in-line skating: street skating and vert skating.

## Street in-line skating

This can be done almost anywhere. Many people skate simply for fun and **recreation**. More aggressive skaters jump over obstacles and grind on the streets and roads, in car parks, along the curb, over benches and picnic tables and down stairways. Skate parks with **ramps** and rails are ideal venues for all types of in-line skating.

Street skating also includes speed skating and slalom.

### Slalom skating

The slalom skater makes sharp, quick turns in and out of a set of cones spaced evenly along a course. The skater tries to avoid knocking over any of the cones. In competition, this will mean a loss of points. Some skaters go backwards through the cones too!

### Speed skating

Speed skating competitions over short or long distances are held on both outdoor and indoor courses.

## Vert in-line skating

Vert skating is done on a huge U-shaped ramp, called a vert ramp or halfpipe. The skater rolls up and back along the ramp, gaining height until a trick can be performed. There are also mini-ramps and quarter-pipes.

## Aggressive in-line skating

This is fast and furious skating by highly skilled skaters. There are both street and vert aggressive in-line skating competitions.

STREET

VERT

# IN-LINE SKATING
# GEAR

## The skates

In-line skaters choose skates that fit well and are comfortable. In-line skates are made up of nine main parts.

### Shell

The shell is the boot to which the wheels are attached. Hard-shell skates are made of hard plastic. A separate liner is placed inside the hard shell. Soft shells are made of synthetic leather and the liner of the boot is sewn into the shell.

Liner

Fastenings

Shell

Wheels

Wheel frame

Heel brake

## Liner

This is the inner boot. The liner is soft and comfortable, and it is padded to support the skater's foot.

## Footbed

The footbed is found inside and at the bottom of the shell. It supports the skater's foot.

## Fastenings

These are the clips, straps, buckles and laces that fasten the skate to the skater's foot.

## Frame

This holds the wheels. The best frames are stiff and light. The heel brake is attached to the back of the frame.

## Heel brake

The heel brake consists of a brake support and a brake pad. It should be fitted to the skate on the skater's strongest leg.

## Wheels

Wheels are made from **urethane** and vary in size and hardness. There are four of them on each skate, but five on a racing skate. Three-wheeled skates are available for beginners and children. Larger, soft wheels give a smooth, fast ride but smaller wheels turn better.

## Bearings

Bearings are found inside the wheels and help them to spin smoothly and quickly. The bearings are precision-made by machine, out of high-quality steel.

## Grind plate

The grind plate is a piece of metal or plastic, fitted to the frame of the skates between the second and third wheels. It helps the skater to perform grinds better.

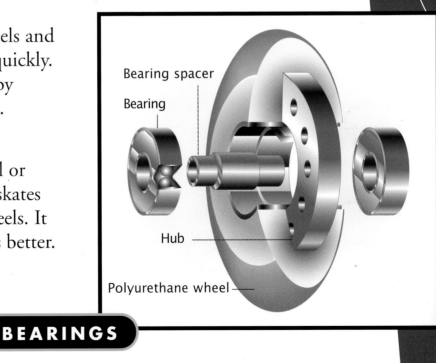

Bearing spacer

Bearing

Hub

Polyurethane wheel

**BEARINGS**

7

# Padding or protective gear

All skaters fall at some time, but those wearing protective equipment are less likely to be injured. Skaters who wear the right protective gear can relax and skate with greater confidence.

**ACTION FACT**

The wrist is the part of the body most often injured by in-line skaters.

### Helmet

Specially designed skating helmets are made of plastic. They are padded with foam to protect the skater's head, particularly the back of the head. (A skater's head is particularly vulnerable during a backwards fall.) Helmets should fit properly and snugly without being tight. All the straps and buckles should lie flat against the skater's head.

### Wrist guards

These are made of hard plastic. They have a splint on both sides to prevent scraped palms and broken or fractured wrists.

### Knee pads

These are made of a strong fabric covered by a hard plastic cup. During a fall, a skater should drop to the knees. This allows the knee pads to absorb the impact of the fall and protect the skater's skin and clothes. The pads should be strapped around the skater's legs firmly to stop them coming off, but not tightly enough to restrict movement.

### Elbow pads

These pads protect elbow joints. Like knee pads, they are made of a strong fabric and are covered by a hard plastic cup.

### Padded shorts or pants

Many skaters also buy padded bike-style shorts for protecting the hips and tailbone. Beginner skaters and aggressive skaters performing tricks wear hip and seat pads for extra protection.

### Appropriate clothes

Most skaters prefer to wear loose and comfortable clothes that allow for plenty of movement. Speed skaters wear clothes that are tight-fitting.

Helmet

Comfortable clothes

Wrist guards

Elbow pads

Knee pads

Padded pants

# Gear for aggressive in-line skaters

Aggressive in-line skating is more dangerous than normal skating, so it requires more protective gear. This gear helps to limit injuries caused by hitting the big ramps and obstacles at high speed while doing street tricks.

The helmet is a hard shell helmet that covers the entire head. The knee and elbow pads are thicker than those worn during regular skating. Wrist guards or fingerless gloves have a wrap-around support strap and at least one splint made of padded leather or **Kevlar**. The baggy shorts are fully padded, and shin guards are commonly worn.

The specially designed shell or boots for aggressive skating are strong enough to support the ankles during high-impact landings. Buckles and cuff hinges are designed with buckle protectors. This stops them catching and causing a crash when the skater slides down rails, or grinds the **coping** or a curb. To allow aggressive in-line skaters to make a safer landing, the frames are flat and have thick, short walls to keep the skater close to the ground. Grind plates are added to the frames to allow the skater to slide along surfaces easily. Aggressive skaters remove the heel brake to prevent it catching on grinding surfaces.

Aggressive in-line skaters wear extra gear for greater protection.

# Gear for speed skaters

Speed skaters must wear a helmet but do not wear the other padding because it slows them down. However, they do wear protective straps on their hands and wrists. Specially designed speed-skating boots have five wheels and lower cuffs. The boots are more flexible at the ankle. This gives skaters greater freedom of movement and allows them to skate with longer strides.

↗ Speed skates have five hard wheels for a faster ride.

# SKATING
# SAFELY

In-line skaters should follow some basic rules to keep themselves safe and free of injury. They should:

- wear light-colored clothing and protective gear (a helmet and wrist, elbow and knee guards)
- choose flat, safe ground on which to learn the basic skills of speed control, turning, braking and stopping
- skate in control at all times
- keep out of traffic by skating in bike lanes on roads or on bicycle tracks

- avoid skating in wet weather
- give way to pedestrians
- obey all road rules
- warn other skaters by calling 'On your right' before passing
- keep skates and protective gear in good working order
- watch out for road hazards
- avoid water, oil and sand.

## FALLING FORWARDS

The skater should try to relax while dropping onto the knee pads, then stretch out onto the wrist pads. The fingers should be kept stretched out in front to avoid injury as the skater slides along on the protective gear.

# Falling safely

All skaters will at some time lose their balance and fall. Falling is part of learning to skate, so skaters must learn how to fall safely. This means that when they fall, they should fall forwards so that they can break the fall with their arms. A backwards fall is dangerous because the head can be injured, even in a helmet.

To avoid falling backwards, the skater must quickly bring the arms to the front, bend the knees and lean forward to touch the knee pads with the hands.

# Getting ready to skate

Gentle stretching, jogging or jumping will warm up and loosen muscles before taking to the skates. Warm, loose muscles work better and are less likely to cramp. Doing some simple exercises before skating may help a skater avoid injury.

**GETTING UP**

The skater rolls onto the knees and kneels on both knees and palms. The skater then moves one leg from the kneeling position to rest the wheels of the skate on the ground. Both hands are placed above the knee for balance.

The skater presses down hard on the knees and stands up. The skater stands still until balanced, then starts off from the V-position, with feet together and toes turned outwards.

# MAINTAINING THE IN-LINE SKATES

Keeping skates in good working order will ensure a safer ride. There are a number of things that skaters can to do to maintain their skates.

## Clean the skates

Skates should be kept clean by being wiped with a damp cloth. After skating, the boots and liners should be allowed to dry out so that bacteria from sweaty feet will be destroyed. This will keep the feet healthy and stop the skates from becoming smelly. Like most protective gear, skate liners can and should be washed.

## Check the brake

The heel brake should be checked often and worn brake pads should be replaced.

## Rotate the wheels

The wheels are worn away by the time spent skating, the skating surface and the force of the skater's weight. Wheels should be rotated every now and again to make sure that the edges wear evenly. Each wheel should be flipped so that the flattened side faces the opposite direction. Wheels from the right skate can be swapped with wheels from the left skate. Rotating the wheels enables them to last longer and gives a smoother, safer ride. Worn wheels should be replaced.

Rotating the wheels ensures that they wear evenly.

# Clean the bearings

The bearings in the wheels should be kept as clean as possible. Dirt, grit and water damage the bearings, and dirty bearings slow down the skates. The bearings should be wiped or brushed after skating. If the bearings are of the type that can be opened and serviced, the casing and ball bearings should be cleaned and oiled lightly.

# A skater's toolkit

Well-prepared skaters carry a small repair kit with them. The toolkit will have:

- allen keys for tightening or removing wheels
- a bearing pusher to push bearings out of the wheel when they need replacing
- spare bearings
- a small Phillips head screwdriver for replacing a brake pad
- an extra heel brake.

Antiseptic cream and a small supply of bandages or sterile gauze are useful additions to the kit.

Extra heel brake

Screwdriver

Bearing pusher

↗ A skater's toolkit.

Allen keys

Spare bearings

# SKILLS, TRICKS AND
# TECHNIQUES

## The basics

Beginner in-line skaters should practice these basic techniques on a safe, flat surface.

### THE READY POSITION

The skater's feet are shoulder-width apart and the toes point forward. Ankles, knees and hips are slightly flexed, the shoulders are forward and the weight is over the balls of the feet. With hands and arms relaxed and head up, the skater looks ahead.

### SCISSORING OR SCISSOR STANCE

Starting from the ready position, the skater shuffles the skates backwards and forwards so that the back wheel of the front skate aligns with the front wheel of the back skate.

### THE V-STANCE, V-WALK AND STROKING

The skater's feet are in a V-position with the heels of the skates almost touching. The skater lifts one foot and places it ahead of the other foot. Then the back foot is raised and placed ahead of the other foot. The feet are always in a V-position and the skater uses the inner edge of the skates. This is sometimes called the duck walk. V-walking on a pavement will have the skater rolling at slow speed. V-walking very quickly is called stroking.

# Stopping

Heel stopping is the best way for an in-line skater to stop, but the T-stop can be used by more experienced skaters. If all else fails, the skater can head for the nearest patch of grass and run onto it!

### HEEL STOP

In-line skates come with a heel brake. To stop, the skater raises the toe of the boot so that the brake scrapes along the ground.

### T-STOP

The heel brake is not used for a T-stop. Instead, the skater turns one foot so that the feet make the shape of a capital T. The skater's knees are bent and the arms are held out to one side.

### TURNING

The skater glides forward with the weight spread equally on both feet, which are held hip-width apart. The skater's arms are relaxed and stretched forward slightly. To turn to the right, the skater bends the left knee to put extra pressure on the front of the left skate, and pushes the left foot out. Pressure on the right skate will turn the skater to the left.

17

# Street in-line skating tricks

Street in-line skating can be done on the streets and roads, or wherever the surface is flat and safe. In skate parks, street skaters use ramps, walls, stairs, boxes and rails of different heights to grind and slide on. The tricks performed by street skaters are a test of balance and help improve the skater's skills.

Grinds can be performed on a curb or railing. There are several different types of grinds. Each one has a specific name, depending on the position of the skater's foot. **Backside**, **frontside** and **shifty** are examples of grinds. A metal or plastic grind plate attached to the skates between the second and third wheels helps with a grind.

## JUMPS

⬈ The jump is the main move for street tricks. A skater learning to jump should wear full protective gear and have friends around to help after a fall.

## GRINDS

⬈ Skating beside a curb or railing, the skater jumps up to land on the curb or railing. The skates are locked onto the landing surface between the second and third wheels.

## GRABS

↙ The skater grabs one skate while the other continues to glide along the rail or curb. In the backside grab, the skater holds the front foot while the back foot grinds along the rail. Grabs can also be performed while the skater is airborne.

## ON THE FUNBOX

↗ Skating up the launch ramp on one side of the funbox, the skater then jumps, **flips** or spins onto the landing ramp. Some funboxes have grind rails for skaters to slide along.

## THE 360 AND THE CAB 360

↗ Skating forwards, the skater jumps into the air and turns a complete circle before landing. This is a 360. A cab 360 involves skating backwards before jumping and turning a complete circle in the air.

# Vert in-line skating tricks

Vert in-line skating is done on huge vert ramps. The skater rolls up and back along the ramp, gaining height until a grind, flip, spin or **air** can be performed.

One of the first things a vert skater learns to do is to pump the vert. This is learning to skate up and down the **transition** of the halfpipe.

Skaters will try to launch themselves into the air above the ramp in order to do tricks. This is called air. The skater who is skilled enough to reach the coping is then ready for some more difficult tricks, such as the 360.

## PUMPING

The skater begins, at the flat on the bottom of the halfpipe, by bending and extending the legs. Moving the arms to gain momentum, the skater pushes up one side of the halfpipe, turns and skates across the flat and then up the other side of the ramp. Gaining speed, the skater gets higher and higher on the ramp.

## AIRS

The 360 and cab 360 can be done as airs. Skating to the top of the ramp, the skater jumps into the air and makes one complete spin before landing. This is the 360. Instead of skating forwards up the ramp, the skater doing a cab 360 skates backwards up the ramp, catches air and makes one complete turn before landing.

## DROPPING-IN

The skater stands with feet placed on the coping or sits at the top of the ramp. The skater then leans forward – drops-in – and rolls down the ramp.

## INVERT TRICKS

The skater reaches the coping and does a handstand by placing one hand on the coping while grabbing the skates with the other hand. After the handstand, the skater's feet are brought down onto the ramp. Then the skater pushes off the coping with the hands and rolls away.

# AN IN-LINE SKATING
# INTERVIEW

Jodie Tyler is an aggressive in-line skate champion who has competed in Australia, the United States and Canada.

## How long have you been an in-line skater?

I have been skating for six years.

## Why did you take it up as a sport?

I took up skating after a friend asked me to go skating one day. Later when I began competing, a lot of professional skaters encouraged me. They were so accepting and helped me learn new tricks.

## What do you like about skating?

I love pushing myself to learn new tricks. It is a constant challenge so I very rarely get bored. Skating is also a very social, fun sport. I have met

people all over the world that are now my friends.

## What sort of people skate in-line?

Anyone can do it. If you want to roll for fitness, anyone at any age can start. There are people who skate after work, people skating for a living, and students.

## What's the atmosphere like at competitions?

The atmosphere at competitions is different to just skating every day. Some people take it very seriously and others are just there for the fun. I enjoy competitions because I get to catch up with friends. I also get to see new tricks that are being done.

## How safe is in-line skating?

In-line skating is mostly a safe sport as long as you learn the basics. Having the right gear and behaving properly on the road will make sure you have an exciting, adventurous and safe time. I've taught at Skate Safe skate clinics where skaters learn about skating safely, correct safety equipment that should be used,

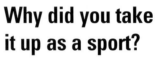

JODIE TYLER

as well as basic tricks. It's a good idea for people who are serious about in-line skating to try to get to one of these clinics. If you are not sure how to do something, ask someone who can teach you the trick. In-line skating on ramps can be dangerous if you are not aware of what you are doing. Before learning, make sure that you have the right safety equipment. Just because some people don't wear all of the right equipment doesn't mean you shouldn't wear it either.

## There are some people who think in-line skaters are a nuisance. What can be done to overcome this problem?

I think education for skaters about being more careful on the streets is one of the keys. Always be aware of people around you and wear the appropriate safety gear. Skaters need to be good role models for the sport. If there isn't a local skate park, approach your city council and try to get them interested in building one that is designed properly by experts.

## How can people find out about the in-line skating scene?

Well, there are books like this one written about in-line skating and there are others that tell how to do it. There are magazines, videos, TV programs, and the internet has sites about in-line skating.

# Career highlights

## 1996
- First place vert, first place street at Cairns Online In-line IISS event
- First place vert, third place street at New York City ASA World Tour
- First place vert at Vancouver ASA World Tour
- Silver medal vert at the X Games in Rhode Island

## 1997
- First place vert, fifth place street at Philadelphia ASA World Tour
- First place female vert in 1997 at Australian In-Line Skating Championships
- First place vert, second place street at Extreme In-Line Series in Canberra, Australia
- First place vert at 1997 Victorian titles in Prahran, Australia

## 1998
- First place female vert at Australian In-Line Skating Championships
- First place vert, fourth place street at Extreme In-Line Series in Canberra, Australia
- First place vert, second place street at 1998 Playstation X-treme Games on the Gold Coast, Australia
- First place vert, equal second street at Vert-X in Penrith, Australia in July
- Third place vert at IISS World Championships in Birmingham, United Kingdom

## 1999
- First place vert at Australian Skate Titles in Canberra, Australia

## 2000
- First place vert, second place street at Australian In-Line Skating Championships

## 2001
- First place vert, first place street at Australian In-Line Skating Championships

# IN COMPETITION

## Street competitions

These are held in an area containing ramps and walls of various heights, and a variety of boxes and rails for sliding and grinding. Competitors skate through a program of jumps, spins, grabs and grinds.

## Ramp or vert competitions

These are performed on a halfpipe. The competitors perform for about 50 seconds each, doing high-flying tricks such as grabs, flips and **inverts**.

## Judging competitions

Judges for both types of competitions are professional skaters or skating experts. They award points on the basis of:

- the number of tricks
- the difficulty of tricks
- the way the skater lands
- line, which is how well the tricks are linked together
- style, which is how good the skater looks while performing.

↗ A vert skater performs on the halfpipe.

## Slalom competition

Slalom is skating around a series of cones placed along a flat course or down a slope. The cones are placed about three feet (one meter) apart. The skater tries to avoid knocking over any of the cones because points are lost for doing so. Points can be won if the skater shows a good skating style or if the skater uses only one foot.

# Speed racing

In-line skaters race outdoors on roads or indoors on tracks made of wood or concrete. Road races are usually held over a distance of 10 kilometers but marathon races covering 26.2 miles are also held. Another outdoor event is the individual time trial. A lone skater races against the clock, rather than against other competitors, for a distance of 300 meters.

Indoor competitions include time trials as well as races of 10 kilometers and 20 kilometers.

# Aggressive skating competitions

In 1994 the Aggressive Skaters Association (ASA) was formed to standardize competitions and promote in-line skating. There are many competitions and the events are televised by the ESPN sports television network. Major competitions include:

- X Games, which are also sponsored by ESPN
- Gravity Games, which began in 1999 and are sponsored by the NBC television network
- National In-line Skate Series (NISS)
- International In-line Skate Series (IISS).

**ACTION FACT**

Some popular 10-kilometer in-line races can have up to 1,000 competitors.

**ACTION FACT**

The fastest in-line skaters are Graham Wilke and Jeff Hamilton, who have both reached a top speed of 64.02 miles (103.03 kilometers) per hour.

Speed racers wear tight clothes and less protective gear.

# IN-LINE SKATING
# CHAMPIONS

In-line skating champions come from all over the world.

## ↗ Cesar Mora

- Vert skater
- Born March 2, 1974, in Madrid, Spain
- Lives in Sydney, Australia
- Began skating in 1993
- Began competing in 1994

### Career highlights

- In 1995, two first places, a second and a third in competitions
- In 1996, three first places, a second and a third in competitions
- In 1997, first place in competitions in Boston, California and Philadelphia, and third place in Australian Championships
- In 1998, first place in competitions
- In 1999, first place in competitions
- In 1999, first person to perform a 1080 degree rotation, which is three complete spins
- In 2000, did a **fakie** 1260 (which is $3\frac{1}{2}$ spins)
- In 2001, ninth place B3 events in California

## ↗ Fabiola Da Silva

- Aggressive in-line skater, street and vert style
- Born June 18, 1979, in Brazil
- Began skating in 1994
- Began competing in 1996

### Career highlights

- In 1996 and 1997, vert competition at the X Games
- In 1998, two first places in X trials, and second in ASA World Championships
- In 1999, both the street and vert competitions at the Gravity Games
- In 2000, first place ASA competition in California, and four first places in B3 events in both street and vert competitions
- In 2001, first place B3 events in the United States

# ↗ Sven Boekhorst

- Aggressive in-line street skater
- Born June 19, 1980, in Holland
- Began skating in 1995
- Began competing in 1997

## Career highlights

- In 1999, two first places in ASA street competitions and first place in Gravity Games
- In 2000, the only skater to have won the top three competitions in the same year – the X Games, the Gravity Games and the Aggressive Skaters Association (ASA) World Championships in Las Vegas
- In 2001, second place street and sixth place vert at the ASA Championships in Rome, Italy

# ↗ Matt Salerno

- Vert skater
- Born April 9, 1978, in Sydney, Australia
- Began skating in 1993
- Began competing in 1995

## Career highlights

- Four times Vert World Champion
- In 1999, ASA World Champion and second place street Extreme Games in Brisbane, Australia
- In 2000, first place vert Gravity Games and first in X trials in Nashville
- In 2001, fourth place park at the X Trials in Texas, and seventh place vert ASA World Team Challenge in California

# THEN AND NOW

| 1700s | 1819 | 1823 | 1863 | 1866 | 1878 | 1884 |
|---|---|---|---|---|---|---|
| A Belgian named Joseph Merlin invented the first roller skates. Merlin was a well-known maker of musical instruments and other mechanical inventions.<br><br>One of the first public showings of his invention was at a fancy dress party in London. Merlin lost control of the skates, crashed into the furniture and broke a mirror! | In France, M. Petitbled developed the first in-line skate. It had wheels on a metal plate with leather straps to attach them to the feet. The wheels were made of wood, metal or ivory. | Englishman Robert John Tyers invented a five-wheeled skate made of iron. | James Leonard Plimpton invented the first modern roller skates. These allowed skaters to turn instead of skating only in a straight line. Plimpton's design is still in use today. | Plimpton opened the first public roller rink in Newport, Rhode Island. It was inside a hotel. | The first official roller hockey game, called roller polo, was played at the Denmark Rink in London, England. | Wheel bearings were invented. These made it easier for skaters to execute turns. |

**1819**

**1863**

| 1890s | 1939 | 1980s | 1988 | 1992 | 1993 | 1997 | 2000 |
|-------|------|-------|------|------|------|------|------|
| Speed skating competitions on banked tracks began in the United States. Events were held in bicycle velodromes. | The first Skate Dance Championship was held at the Mineola Rink in New York. | The first modern in-line skate was developed by two brothers in the United States, Scott and Brennan Olson. The brothers were ice-hockey players from Minnesota who wanted to practice their skating in the summer. They called their in-line skates Rollerblades. | More than 1 million pairs of the Rollerblade brand of in-line skates had been sold in the United States. | Roller hockey became an exhibition sport in the Summer Olympic Games in Barcelona, Spain. | The number of in-line skaters around the world was estimated at more than 25 million. | Skates for in-line figure skating were designed. | In-line skating versions of soccer and basketball became popular. |

1992

2000

# RELATED ACTION
# SPORTS

### Roller hockey

Two teams of four players plus a goalie play four 12-minute quarters. The aim of the game is to hit the puck (a ball) into the net, past the opposing team's goalie.

### Downhill

This in-line skating sport was developed from downhill skiing. There are two types of races: slalom races (skating around cones) and downhill races.

### Roller soccer and roller basketball

These are in-line skate versions of two well-known and popular sports.

## FREESTYLE

In-line figure skaters jump, turn and do aerial spins, the features of figure skating on ice. Freestyle also includes street dancing.

## CROSS-COUNTRY SKATING

Skaters charge across the countryside, jumping over rocks and other obstacles. They wear in-line skates with larger wheels and no brakes.

# GLOSSARY

**air** a jump involving time in the air when skates do not have contact with anything

**backside** a grind using only the back foot

**coping** the metal bar at the top edge of the halfpipe

**fakie** landing backwards

**flip** any move in which the skater is upside down

**frontside** a type of grind

**grind** a move in which the skater jumps onto something and slides down it on skates

**halfpipe** a U-shaped ramp, usually made of wood or metal. Also called a vert ramp or mini-ramp

**invert** a movement in which the skater goes upside down on the ramp and does a handstand; usually done on the coping of the halfpipe

**Kevlar** an artificial material that is extremely strong and heat-resistant

**ramp** usually refers to a halfpipe, but can be a quarter-pipe or launch ramp

**recreation** something done for fun, not competition

**shifty** a grind on the inside edge of one skate, and on the outside edge of the trailing skate; also known as a royale

**skate park** a specially designed and built venue for in-line skating

**transition** the part of a ramp that goes from horizontal to vertical

**urethane** a tough plastic used to make in-line skate wheels

**vert** the vertical section at the top of the ramp

31

# INDEX